Visit the
GREAT BASIN

By Kathryn Walton

Enslow
PUBLISHING

Please visit our website, www.enslow.com. For a free color catalog of all our high-quality books, call toll free 1-800-398-2504 or fax 1-877-980-4454.

Library of Congress Cataloging-in-Publication Data
Names: Walton, Kathryn, 1993- author.
Title: Visit the Great Basin / Kathryn Walton.
Description: Buffalo, NY : Enslow Publishing, [2024] | Series: Visit
    America's regions! | Includes bibliographical references and index.
Identifiers: LCCN 2023033115 (print) | LCCN 2023033116 (ebook) | ISBN
    9781978537484 (library binding) | ISBN 9781978537477 (paperback) | ISBN
    9781978537491 (ebook)
Subjects: LCSH: Great Basin–Juvenile literature.
Classification: LCC F789 .W35 2024 (print) | LCC F789 (ebook) | DDC
    917.9–dc23/eng/20230803
LC record available at https://lccn.loc.gov/2023033115
LC ebook record available at https://lccn.loc.gov/2023033116

Published in 2024 by
Enslow Publishing
2544 Clinton Street
Buffalo, NY 14224

Portions of this work were originally authored by Kathleen Connors and published as *Let's Explore The Great Basin*.
All new material in this edition is authored by Kathryn Walton.

Designer: Claire Wrazin
Editor: Natalie Humphrey

Photo credits: Series art (leather spine and corners) nevodka/Shutterstock.com, (map) Karin Hildebrand Lau/Shutterstock.com, (stamped boxes) lynea/Shutterstock.com, (old paper) Siam SK/Shutterstock.com, (vintage photo frame) shyshak roman/Shutterstock.com, (visitor's guide paper background) Andrey_Kuzmin/Shutterstock.com; cover, p. 1 (main) Bryan Chernick/Shutterstock.com; cover, p. 1 (Salt Lake City) Charles E Uibel/ Shutterstock.com; p. 5 (United States map) pingebat/Shutterstock.com, (striped pattern) Oleh Svetiukha/Shutterstock.com; p. 7 (sagebrush) FtLaud/Shutterstock.com, (rabbitbrush) Carol Provins/Shutterstock.com; p. 9 Surelocke/Shutterstock.com; p. 11 Virrage Images/Shutterstock. com; p. 13 (top) Rachel Doreen/Shutterstock.com; p. 13 (bottom) Jason Finn/Shutterstock.com; p. 14 Kelly vanDellen/Shutterstock.com; p. 15 photos4uuuu/Shutterstock.com; p. 17 (left) CHRISTIAN DE ARAUJO/Shutterstock.com; p. 17 (right) tusharkoley/Shutterstock.com; p. 19 Michael Vi/Shutterstock.com; p. 21 Cavan-Images/Shutterstock.com.

CPSIA compliance information: Batch #CWENS24: For further information contact Enslow Publishing at 1-800-398-2504.

Find us on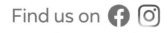

CONTENTS

Words in the glossary appear in **bold** type the first time they are used in the text.

WELCOME TO THE GREAT BASIN!

The Great **Basin** is an area of nearly 200,000 square miles (518,000 square km) in the western United States. Most of Nevada and Utah are part of the Great Basin. Smaller areas of Oregon, Idaho, Wyoming, and California are included as well.

The Great Basin is bordered by the Sierra Nevada mountain range to the west. To the east are the Wasatch Mountains. To the north is the Snake River Plain, and to the south is the Mojave Desert.

• VISITOR'S GUIDE •

THE GREAT BASIN IS AN AREA OF LAND IN WHICH THE CREEKS, STREAMS, AND RIVERS DON'T CONNECT TO THE OCEAN. INSTEAD, THE WATER **EVAPORATES**, GOES UNDERGROUND, OR FLOWS INTO LAKES.

GREAT BASIN

A COLD DESERT

Most of the Great Basin is a cold desert. Cold deserts are often at a higher **elevation** than most other deserts.

Only about 6 to 12 inches (15 to 30.5 cm) of **precipitation** falls each year in the Great Basin. The towering mountains of the Sierra Nevada and Cascade Range often keep rain from reaching the area. The plants and animals that live in the Great Basin have **adapted** to the weather.

• VISITOR'S GUIDE •

SNOW IS THE ONLY FORM OF PRECIPITATION IN THE COLD DESERT PARTS OF THE GREAT BASIN.

Plants like sagebrush and rabbitbrush are found all over the Great Basin's cold desert. They can survive without much water and are often eaten by the animals there.

SAGEBRUSH

RABBITBRUSH

7

THE PEOPLE OF THE GREAT BASIN

Native Americans have lived in the Great Basin for a long time. **Archaeologists** believe the Washoe people have been living in Nevada for thousands of years! The Western Shoshone, Ute, Washoe, and Paiute peoples are just some of the Native groups that still live in the Great Basin.

Many museums in the Great Basin area, such as the Nevada State Museum, have ancient **artifacts** from these peoples on display. Museums are buildings where people can see things of interest.

• VISITOR'S GUIDE •

IN EASTERN UTAH, YOU CAN VISIT NINE MILE CANYON. NINE MILE CANYON IS AROUND 46 MILES (74 KM) LONG AND FEATURES OVER 10,000 PIECES OF NATIVE AMERICAN ROCK ART.

CROSSING THE GREAT BASIN

In the late 1700s, fur trappers and **explorers** found the Great Basin hard to cross. Then, in 1844, an explorer named John C. Frémont mapped much of the area. His work, in addition to the California gold rush starting in 1849, brought more people to the Great Basin.

In 1862, the U.S. government passed the Homestead Act, which gave land to settlers willing to farm it for five years. This also drew people to the Great Basin **region**.

Today, travelers can drive across the Great Basin using Interstate 80.

SALT LAKE CITY

Salt Lake City, Utah, is one of the biggest cities in the Great Basin. Visitors can see the Utah Olympic Oval and Olympic Cauldron Park. This is where some of the events of the 2002 Olympic Winter Games took place.

The Great Salt Lake is one of the most popular places to visit. This lake is not only the largest saltwater lake in the western half of the world, it's also saltier than Earth's oceans!

• VISITOR'S GUIDE •

IN 1847, BRIGHAM YOUNG LED 147 PEOPLE TO THE PLACE WHERE SALT LAKE CITY WAS FOUNDED. HE WAS LOOKING FOR A PLACE TO FREELY PRACTICE HIS FAITH AS PART OF THE CHURCH OF JESUS CHRIST OF LATTER-DAY SAINTS.

All the salt in the Great Salt Lake makes it easier for people to float!

DEATH VALLEY

One of the lowest parts of the Great Basin is called Death Valley. Death Valley got its name in 1849 because it was so hard for people to cross. It's no wonder—Death Valley is the lowest, driest, and hottest place in all of North America! During the summer, Death Valley can be as hot as 120°F (49°C) during the day.

Today, Death Valley National Park is a popular place in the Great Basin. The park is in southeastern California.

Death Valley National Park

Homeland of the Timbisha Shoshone

DEATH VALLEY
NATIONAL PARK

It only rains around
2 inches (5 cm) each year
in Death Valley.

• VISITOR'S GUIDE •

DEATH VALLEY NATIONAL PARK INCLUDES BADWATER
BASIN, WHICH IS 282 FEET (86 M) BELOW
SEA LEVEL, AND TELESCOPE PEAK, WHICH IS MORE
THAN 11,000 FEET (3,353 M) HIGH.

RENO, NEVADA

Reno, Nevada, is another of the largest cities in the Great Basin. Reno is known for its many **casinos** and flashy live shows. It's been drawing crowds since 1931, and today, over 270,000 people live in Reno.

Reno's famous **arch** lights up over the downtown casinos and reads, "The Biggest Little City in the World." The original arch was built in 1926, before the casinos. The arch was built to mark the first cross-country road routes!

The current Reno sign looks much different than the one built in 1926.

ANOTHER POPULAR VACATION SPOT IN THE GREAT BASIN REGION IS LAKE TAHOE. TO THE SOUTHWEST OF RENO ON THE BORDER OF CALIFORNIA, LAKE TAHOE IS THE SECOND-DEEPEST LAKE IN THE UNITED STATES!

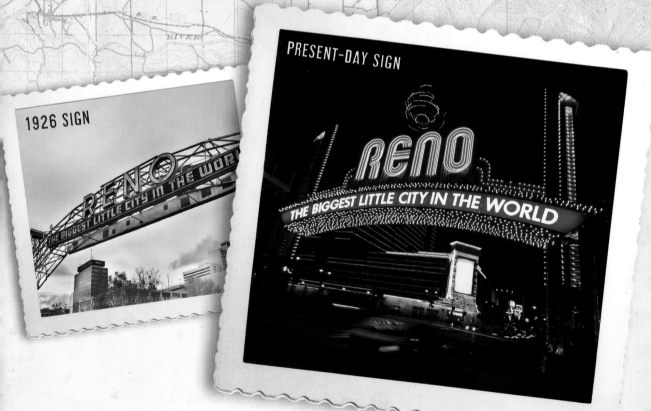

1926 SIGN

PRESENT-DAY SIGN

THE COMSTOCK LODE

In 1859, people found a huge amount of silver in Nevada. This find, known as the Comstock Lode, brought people from around the country to mine in Nevada. Several towns popped up to support these miners. Many of these towns were abandoned, or left behind by the owners. But some towns, like Virginia City, are still around today.

Mining is still important in the Great Basin region. Nevada produces more gold than any other U.S. state!

Because silver was so important to the state's history, Nevada is also called the "silver state."

• VISITOR'S GUIDE •

THE RICHES OF THE COMSTOCK LODE HELPED
LEAD THE U.S. GOVERNMENT TO MAKE NEVADA
A STATE IN 1864.

THE

COMSTOCK LODE

DISCOVERED 8 JUNE 1859

AT HEAD OF SIX MILE CANYON
WASHOE MINING DISTRICT
VIRGINIA CITY, NEVADA

THIS MONUMENT OF ORE FROM
EVERY NEVADA COUNTY
COMMEMORATES THE ONE-
HUNDREDTH ANNIVERSARY OF
THE DISCOVERY OF SILVER.

GREAT BASIN NATIONAL PARK

Visiting Great Basin National Park is one of the best ways to see many of the things the Great Basin has to offer! Visitors can hike the many paths through the mountains in the Great Basin. You can even go camping in different places around the park.

Great Basin National Park was **established** on October 27, 1986. Like other national parks, Great Basin National Park is protected. This means that the land, plants, and animals in the park are kept safe by U.S. laws.

GREAT BASIN
NATIONAL PARK

UNITED STATES DEPARTMENT OF THE INTERIOR / NATIONAL PARK SERVICE

NATIONAL PARK SERVICE

In 2021, over 144,000 people visited Great Basin National Park.

• VISITOR'S GUIDE •

GREAT BASIN NATIONAL PARK IS ALSO A DARK SKY SITE. THIS IS A PLACE WHERE MANMADE LIGHT IS VERY CONTROLLED. DARK SKY SITES ARE THE BEST PLACES TO SEE THE STARS!

GLOSSARY

adapt: To change to suit conditions.

arch: A structure built in the shape of a curve.

archaeologist: A scientist who studies past human life and activities.

artifact: Something made by humans in the past.

basin: A dip in Earth's surface, shaped somewhat like a bowl.

casino: A place where people play games of chance to try to win money.

elevation: Height above sea level.

establish: To create something.

evaporate: To change from a liquid to a gas.

explorer: A person who searches to find out new things.

precipitation: Rain, snow, sleet, or hail.

region: A large area of land that has features that make it different from nearby areas of land.

FOR MORE INFORMATION

Books

Gagne, Tammy. *Death Valley*. New York, NY: AV2, 2021.

Sebra, Richard. *Nevada*. Minneapolis, MN: Core Library, 2023.

Websites

Great Basin National Park
www.nps.gov/grba/index.htm
Learn more about visiting the Great Basin and how to plan your trip from the National Park Service.

Native People of the American Great Basin
kids.nationalgeographic.com/history/article/native-people-of-the-american-great-basin
Learn more about the people native to the Great Basin.

INDEX